KINGDOM
MINISTRY

KINGDOM MINISTRY

*Walking in the
Power of Service*

John Wimber

HODDER AND STOUGHTON
LONDON SYDNEY AUCKLAND TORONTO

British Library Cataloguing in Publication Data

Wimber, John
  Kingdom ministry.
  1. Christian life.
  I. Title
  248.4

  ISBN 0 340 48864 6

*Hodder and Stoughton Editorial Office: 47 Bedford Square, London
WC1B 3DP*

KINGDOM MINISTRY

Do you ever go through times when you lose sight of God's purpose for your life? I do. Usually this happens to me when I get caught up in ministry concerns but lose sight of my source for service: Jesus Christ. When I do this, God reminds me gently but firmly that I have been called to serve him first.

Not too long ago, I was preparing to leave my home for a few days' holiday. I needed the rest and recreation. I had been working very hard for weeks, ministering to an endless line of people, folks with insurmountable problems. The thought of being inconvenienced by another human being was too much for me to handle. I had to get away.

But before I could leave, the phone rang once more. Reluctantly, I picked it up. It was a member of my congregation who was hurting badly, and God wanted me to help her. I had to serve again, right then, and I didn't like it. I hung up the phone and stormed out of the back door of my house. I looked up at the sky. I didn't exactly shake my fist at God, but I threw my hands up in the air, palms inward, like an Italian merchant who had just taken delivery of a shipment of damaged goods.

"Who do you think you are?" I roared.

Lightning didn't strike me dead, although I deserved to die for my impertinence. I spent two days repenting for my sin. God was God. I was a creature, created to do his bidding.

During this time of repentance, the Lord led me to a scripture passage that had long puzzled me. It was Luke 17:7–10. In this text, Jesus is teaching the disciples about faith and forgiveness and repentance. Suddenly, he shifts gears and starts talking about being servants.

Say you have a servant, he tells his disciples. The two of you are out all day working in the fields or tending the flocks. The end of the day comes, and the two of you return to the house tired, dirty, and hungry.

"Will you say to him, 'Come at once and sit down at the table?'" asks Jesus. The question is obviously rhetorical. Of course the master wouldn't tell the servant to sit down at the table. Jesus goes on.

"Will he not rather say to him, 'Prepare supper for me, and gird yourself and serve me, till I eat and drink; and afterward you shall eat and drink?' Does he thank the servant because he did what was commanded?" Again, the question is obviously rhetorical. Of course the master wouldn't treat his servant this way.

Jesus moves on to the point of his little story: "So you also, when you have done all that is commanded you, say, 'We are unworthy servants; we have only done what was our duty.'"

This passage is difficult for us Americans to understand because equality of personhood, not respect of authority, is highly valued in our society. The master looks arrogant, sitting there alone at the table while his tired and hungry servant serves him dinner. Why couldn't he ask his servant to join him? At least he should have let him take a shower first.

But I wept when I read this passage. Why should I be excused from taking care of a woman in my church who was in bad trouble? Because I was tired and wanted a day off? Because I wanted a night out? People with troubles are to be expected in ministry. My problem was not created by this woman but by my compulsive work habits. Taking care of the people in my flock is nothing more than my duty, my calling, what God placed me here on earth to do. Should I get a medal every time I do what I'm supposed to do?

Of course not. Jesus' disciples had plenty of trouble understanding what it meant to be a servant, but at least they quickly understood that a servant serves. He does what he's told. He fulfils his duty.

Embracing the Call

Too often we not only forget our duty, we lose sight of the very call that first prompted us to be a servant of God. This is the plight of many of us, especially pastors. Because of massive responsibilities, we get lured away from the very things that are central to Christian service.

I have talked with countless pastors who have become almost completely ineffective in personal witnessing. When they were called to serve Christ in their youth, they were effective at winning people to Christ. As their ministry and responsibilities expanded, they became entangled in the demands of leadership and forgot their first call. Acts 1:8 says we are to be witnesses. This is true for lay and ordained persons alike.

My friend Michael Green, formerly Vicar of St. Aldate's Church in Oxford, England and now a professor of evangelism at Regent College in Vancouver, B.C., is one of the few professionals who have held fast to their early ministry to personal evangelism. I admire him most not because of his position or the many fine books he has written. Not because he is one of the finest preachers I've heard, nor because he is an effective leader. I admire him most because every week he goes out into the marketplace in order to win people to Christ. Michael is an example of a man who has embraced the call to servanthood in its fullness. He hasn't ignored one aspect of ministry for the sake of another. You see, God calls us to be faithful in each of our duties, no excuses made.

Jesus is Lord. We are his servants. He is master. We do what he tells us to do.

"Jesus is my Lord," we say. "I am the Lord's servant." The words pass easily, glibly, from our lips.

But I think we rarely understand what these words really mean. Too often, being a servant in the church today means getting ahead, manipulating others, doing what we want to do. Being a servant means little more than dressing up some very worldly modes of behaviour in "religious" language.

If you don't understand what it means to be a servant, or if you do understand but fail to act that way, be consoled. You are in the best company. Jesus taught the apostles how to serve by word and example during three years of intimate personal contact. Yet the apostles so thoroughly and so consistently failed to grasp what he meant that the spectacle is almost comical.

In particular, the apostles failed to recognise Jesus' intention to establish a spiritual kingdom on earth. They assumed Jesus was talking about establishing a political kingdom – and they were going to be the new masters! This misunderstanding, combined with their personal ambition, was deadly. It created a formidable barrier to their understanding that servanthood means being servants, not lords.

For three years, Jesus taught about the Kingdom of God. For three years, the apostles understood him to mean a worldly kingdom. They looked forward to throwing their weight around in this kingdom. They probably thought about how they would reward their friends, settle old scores with their enemies, and set up their relatives in good jobs once the kingdom came.

We know for a fact that they jockeyed among themselves for good positions.

This rivalry broke into the open one day when the mother of James and John had the gall to ask Jesus if he could please set one of her boys at his right and the other at his left in the kingdom. The other apostles were indignant when they heard about it, but I'll bet it was because the woman asked first, not because they understood what the kingdom was really all about. I can imagine them saying to each other, "Did you hear what Jim and Johnny's mother did? Did you ever see such *chutzpah*?"

They all wanted to be important officials in the kingdom – under Jesus, of course.

Jesus used this occasion to patiently explain the difference between service in the Kingdom of God and worldly authority in the secular realm.

He began with the model of leadership they were most familiar with. "You know that the rulers of the Gentiles lord it over them," he said, "and their great men exercise authority over them."

The apostles certainly knew this. The Romans had installed a puppet king over Israel, were shipping off the olive oil and figs and wine of the land, were taxing the people until they bled, and were hampering their religious observances. A crop of ambitious Jewish sycophants, flatterers, and fellow-travellers had sprung up around the court of these pagan tyrants like mushrooms in a damp dark basement. Even the reformers – the Pharisees – were after power. They wanted to gain control of the religious life of the people.

Yes, the apostles knew all about rulers who "lord it over them". We know all about them, too. In fact, we in the twentieth century do tyranny a lot more efficiently and ruthlessly than the Romans did.

To this model, Jesus contrasts his own.

"It shall not be so among you," he said. "But whoever would be great among you must be your servant, and whoever would be first among you must be your slave."

Jesus ends by offering himself as the new model:

"Even as the Son of man came not to be served but to serve, and to give his life as a ransom for many" (Mt 20:28).

This sounds attractive, doesn't it? We become Christians and make a clean break with all those ugly worldly authorities – the money-grubbing con men with whom we have to do business, the ambitious politicians, the un-reasonable bosses we work for, the bloodthirsty tyrants who oppress most of the people in the world. We replace all this with leadership as service. Helping other people. Being nice. Doing what the Lord wants done. Serving.

Sound easy?

No, not really. It must be hard. Not many of us serve the way Jesus did and then commanded us to do. I don't. I don't see many people in the churches who do. Most of us do fairly worldly jobs in church and call them "service" and adopt a worldly role and call it "servant". The radical transforming power of the Lord hasn't penetrated. We don't want it to.

When the Lord began to radically change my way of pastoring back in the late 1970s, he started with my concept of being a servant. At the time I was perceived as an expert in church growth. I would fly all over the country telling ministers how to boost their numbers and double church income. I was good at what I did. People praised me for it. I thought God must like it, too. I was doing a lot for him – as his servant, of course. And the job paid well.

I was no brutal tyrant. I didn't impose my

will with a heavy hand. I didn't think I was a Sadducee or a Roman governor. I saw myself as a servant of the church.

Nevertheless, I was a young man on the move. I marketed myself as someone who could show churches how to grow – and in itself that wasn't a bad thing. Winning people to Christ and adding them to the local church is good. The problem wasn't with what I did; it was with my motivation. I wanted to be a success and find my identity in my success. I was serving myself, not my Master, and spiritually it wore me down. Because of this I became preoccupied with measuring numerical and financial growth. The more people and money churches had, I thought, the more successful I am.

But eventually the Lord showed me how wrong this was. I became worn out, because ministry motivated by personal ambition runs on human power, not divine anointing. In obedience to him, I stopped doing the church growth seminars. I packed up my ring binders and flip charts, went home, and waited for my next ministry to emerge. And waited. And waited.

"Time's wasting, Lord. When do I start calling on people, telling about you?" I said.

"Come before me," he said.

"Lord, I'm an evangelical. Don't you know what an evangelical is? I'm called to evangelise. That's the highest need of the church."

"Get rid of your office and shut off your telephone," he said. "Worship me. Cry a lot."

The Lord led me to the story of Martha and Mary. I'd always disliked this story. Mary was one of my least favourite people in the Bible.

"She's a wimp, Lord," I complained. "I don't like people who sit around and do nothing. I'm an activist. I've got things to do and people to see."

"Am I among them?" he asked.

"Well, sure, Lord. You're among them. I'm doing this all for you."

"No, you're not. You're doing it for *you*. You want to be a success."

That stung me. The word of God cut right down to the marrow that time. I could see that the Lord was right. I wanted to make it in this career I was in – the career of big-time evangelist. I looked back on my life and began to understand what the Lord had done for me and where I stood in relation to him.

He had saved me. At the age of 29 I was on the road to hell. The Lord confronted me and called me to himself. In the years since, my marriage got better, my kids got straightened out, my family prospered, and other blessings showered down in great abundance. But none of that was promised to me the night I knelt on my best friend's living room floor and sobbed my guts out in thanksgiving. It was enough to be saved. I don't think anyone even mentioned heaven that night. They just said I didn't have to carry my sin any more. I was so glad to get rid of it.

How did this miracle come about? I realised I couldn't handle my life anymore. I asked Jesus to become Lord of it.

And what did that mean?

It meant that he was *Lord*. I wasn't. That was the whole point. I asked *him* to be Lord of my life because I had made a mess of the job, didn't want to do it, couldn't do it. I was a servant, an underling, a fellow who took instructions and relied on the master's power to see that the orders were carried out.

Serving God's Purposes

Sometimes when I stroll through a Christian bookstore or hear some preachers on TV, I wonder why everyone doesn't become a Christian. The Christianity package includes material prosperity, a better marriage, pious kids, better time management, a better sex life, a budget that works, a self-image that will knock your socks off, and godly grooming and skin care. These benefits really are showered on Christians often enough. Why doesn't everyone in the world line up to get theirs?

Because all these benefits are beside the point. We are here to serve his purposes, not our own. Some of us are blessed materially. Some of us aren't. Some have better marriages after their conversion. Some don't. But every Christian must make Jesus the Lord of his or her life. We've been saved from eternal death, not to follow our own fancies, but to do his will and his purposes.

It's hard to do this. Fortunately, the Lord has given us the ability to be faithful servants. He gives us the Holy Spirit to guide and empower us. But it's also a fact that the very act of conversion to Christ frees us from the slavery to old models and passions.

Again and again I have had to root out of my life old habits, passions, and desires in order to assume the proper posture before the master. Just recently I found myself in a convention centre waiting to address several thousand people. As I sat on the podium among the other ministers, I had a pleasant moment of reflection in which I thought to myself, "Lord, this is good. I am glad you brought me here. I am glad to be among these brethren. It's good of you, Lord, to open these kinds of doors for me."

Immediately the Lord spoke to me, "I didn't bring you here." I was incredibly shocked. I was frightened.

"You didn't bring me here?" I spoke aloud, unable to suppress my shock.

"What did you say?" asked the person sitting next to me.

"Oh, nothing."

But, frankly, I had begun to perspire profusely. I spoke under my breath, "Lord, you didn't bring me here?"

"No," he answered.

"Then why am I here?"

"It's the same old thing, John. You're still trying to find an identity. You're still trying to find a father other than me."

I began to weep. "Lord, I don't want any father but you. I don't want any other relationship but the one I have with you."

"Then listen to me and not to men."

God had put his finger on the issue. I had accepted this invitation because I knew it would be something that would enable me to gain approval from others. In fact, the people who had invited me had placed significant pressure on me to convince me to come. I had realised that they would be insulted if I didn't accept their invitation. I complied so that I could "keep the peace".

As I sat there, it became painfully evident to me that I had somehow taken my eyes off the Father and was looking again to men to make me comfortable, to give me identity and purpose.

"Oh, God, forgive me," I repented.

"I have," he answered. "Don't worry, I'm not going to abandon you. You're going to do well here tonight. But next time you receive an invitation to something, let's talk about it."

Our Relationship to God

I live in Southern California. In that part of the country there is no more fitting time to have a dialogue with God and learn important spiritual truths than while driving down the freeway. That's the place where I learned about the status my conversion to Christ had conferred on me.

This dialogue occurred while I was struggling with the new ministry I wanted, but which the Lord seemed to be keeping from me. As I was driving, the Lord began to show me all the conversions I had experienced in my life. The first was my conversion to Pall Mall cigarettes when I was 13. There was a succession of others: to music, to several different styles of life, to groups of people, to an ideal of success, to a certain pattern of relationships.

A common thread ran through all of these conversions. I had done each out of a desire to be successful, to be known, to *become* someone. A terrible thought surfaced: did I convert to Jesus Christ for the same reason, to become someone?

Then the Lord spoke.

"John, when are you going to believe that you *are* someone? I made you someone. I purchased you with my blood. I've called you to be mine. Stop worrying about who you are."

I was so overcome with emotion that I pulled to the side of the road and opened my Bible. I opened to Matthew 3 – the story of the baptism of Jesus. My finger fell on the Father's words: "This is my beloved Son in whom I am well pleased." I was puzzled.

"I don't understand, Lord."

"That's the point. You don't understand. How much service had I given my Father up to that point?"

"None, Lord."

"That's right. And *already* he was well pleased."

I had known the Lord for fourteen years and I had always been looking for approval from him. Now I realised that approval came from the relationship I had with him, not from the work I did. The key is the relationship. Jesus had a relationship with the Father. I have a relationship with Jesus. The essence of these relationships is the same: master and servant.

At last I understood.

What does a servant do? The easy answer is to say that a servant serves. He does what the master wants done. Jesus is the king. All creation is subject to him. A king with a realm this large has many things he needs done. We do this work.

And what is this work? There is a terribly inflated mystique about "service" in the church today. "The Lord's work" tends to get identified with highly visible "ministries" of teaching, preaching, and church planting; with being an elder, pastor, or counsellor; with exercising spiritual gifts such as prophecy and healing.

The truth is that the Lord's work is humble caring. Everybody should serve this way, and should do so gladly.

Deeds over Words

Mother Teresa has taught me much about the whole idea of servanthood. She is a woman who has spent many years tending the needs of the poorest of the poor in the streets of Calcutta and throughout the world. Her service is not characterised by a lot of preaching or proclamation of the gospel, but she displays the gospel of deeds over and against the gospel of words.

In her care for abandoned babies, for those who are dying, and for those who are impoverished, she has communicated the truth that there is indeed a God of mercy and holiness in the world who is willing to reach out and touch people. Mother Teresa is a servant in every classic sense of the scriptural term. She has given herself, not only to the service of the poor, but she has also been able to rally others who would do the same.

It seems to me that one of the key lessons that Mother Teresa has learned is how to be single-hearted in her ministry. Often, when approached by others who are merely curious about the nature of her ministry, she responds with the simple phrase – "Come and see". She wants to put service first before spending a lot of time explaining her ministry to others.

Her witness has on numerous occasions convicted me as I have caught myself doing just the opposite. I have found myself drawn into untenable positions as I try to explain a ministry which God has given to us that can't be fully explained to anyone other than to those who receive it.

Imitating Jesus

We learn how to be servants of the master by imitating the way our master serves *his* Lord. Jesus did the Father's bidding on earth. The Father's will is *all* he did. He spent many hours in solitary prayer seeking the Father's will and he lived a life of total dedication to his service.

One of the best portraits of Jesus the servant is found in the second chapter of Philippians. Here Paul describes the indescribable self-emptying of God become man.

Christ Jesus, who, though he was in the form of God, did not count equality with God a thing to be grasped, but emptied himself, taking the form of a servant, being born in the likeness of men. And being found in human form he humbled himself and became obedient unto death, even death on a cross.

The word translated "servant" could also be translated "slave". Read the passage again with that word and think about it. Jesus came as a slave. It's bad enough to be a servant, but at least servants have some rights. Servants get paid. They can quit. They can file a grievance about working conditions with the shop steward of the servants' union. But slaves have *no* rights. They are *owned* by the master they serve.

When God became man, he came as a slave.

Think about that.

He even led a slave's life, virtually devoid of the "blessings" the books say Christians should enjoy. He was estranged from his family. He was celibate and had no family of his own. He had no education, no wealth or property, no status, no home. He spent the last three years of his life as a wanderer with no place to lay his head. He died a squalid criminal's death. He lived and died this way in obedience to his Father's will.

Here is your model for your service as a servant.

And what is this service? Read the verses that precede this description of Jesus. Paul writes about how Christians are to relate to each other.

"Complete my joy by being of the same

mind, having the same love, being in full accord and of one mind," he writes.

Does this sound like your church? Your Bible study group? Your home? It doesn't? In the next verse, Paul tells us how to achieve oneness of mind: "Do nothing from selfishness or conceit, but in humility count others better than yourselves."

The "humility" that Paul refers to here is not a grovelling concession that everyone else is more gifted, more beautiful, and more worthwhile than you are. It refers to status. The servants in God's household treat everyone else as if they had higher status in the kingdom. A servant takes care of others first, then himself. The essence of servanthood is to live out your life for someone else. That's the kind of life Jesus led. That's the kind of life we are called to.

Other-Centred

This is what ministry is – serving and caring for others. In our fellowship I will often tell someone to "minister" to someone in need. "What will I say?" he or she will often ask. "I don't have any good advice to give them." Usually I will say something like: "Don't say anything, just take care of them. Hug them. Cry with them. Laugh with them. Get them a dinner. Mow their lawn. Fix their car. That's ministry."

Ministry means doing whatever is necessary to help others overcome their problems and grow in confidence and holiness. We grow like plants. When you minister to someone you tend them like you tend a garden. The ministry of a servant has a lot more in common with the nurse-patient or parent-child relationship than it does with the social worker-client or psychotherapist-neurotic relationship that are so often the models for "ministry" in the church.

The truth is that ministry is much more than wise counsel and inspired prayer. It includes these things, but most of the most important and necessary kinds of ministry are simple practical stuff. Listening. Babysitting. Driving people around town. Ministry means taking care of people, putting them first. Ministry is the work of a servant. It's simple work but also hard work because it means putting yourself in the back seat, and that is never easy.

Talents: Use Them or Lose Them

If you think you are too ordinary and too humble to do anything for the Kingdom, go to Matthew 25 and reread the parable of the talents. This is the parable for the modest, apprehensive, ordinary Christian. It's for every man and woman who gets tongue-tied when eloquence is needed, who feels like running when that disturbed person comes in the door, who is convinced that he or she isn't bright enough, doesn't know the Bible well enough, and doesn't have enough time to help anybody.

Remember the story?

The master is going away for a while. He entrusts his property to three servants. One gets five talents; the second gets two; the third gets one. The master makes the division according to the servants' abilities.

The more able servants do well. The most gifted servant wheels and deals, gets up early to read the *Wall Street Journal*, spends hours on the phone with his broker every day, gets into the best tax shelters, and manages to double his master's money. His five talents become ten, and the master is delighted.

The second servant has less money to work with and is less sharp as an investor. He probably put the money in a safe but profitable portfolio of tax-free municipals, blue chip stocks, and money markets. But he doubled his money too. The master was very pleased to get four talents back when he returned.

The third servant was afraid. As soon as his master left, the poor guy rushed off and buried his one talent in the ground. Years later, when the master asked for an explanation, the little guy explained that he didn't want to take any chances.

"You are a hard man," he told the master. "I didn't want to make any mistakes. Here's your one talent back, good as the day you gave it to me."

"You bet I'm a hard man," the master said. "You could have at least put my money in a savings account and got a little interest. Your fear got the better of you and that shows that you are an unworthy servant."

If you aren't doing anything to serve the Lord because you are afraid of screwing up, making mistakes, and looking like a fool, watch out. You are eventually going to have to account for your stewardship to God, and that's *really* something to be afraid of. Even if you have only one talent, or even half a talent, the master expects you to use it. Use it or lose it. The choice is yours.

The Faithful Servant

What are the greatest attributes of a servant? The parable of the talents seems to suggest that the master prizes resourcefulness and crafty dealing. But look again.

The master praises and rewards the first two servants in the same way: "Well done, good and faithful servant; you have been faithful *over a little*, I will set you over much." (Emphasis added.) The servants are rewarded for their *faithfulness*, not for their shrewd investment. Multiplying their master's property was no more than their job. They were rewarded because they did their job, not because they got their master into some nice oil and gas deals and made him rich.

The best thing a servant can do is to be faithful. "It is required of stewards that they be found trustworthy," writes Paul to the rebellious and complaining Corinthians. Paul salutes the Ephesian Christians by calling them "faithful in Christ Jesus". When Barnabas, representing the elders in Jerusalem, paid the first official visit to the church in Antioch, he exhorted them all "to remain faithful to the Lord with steadfast purpose."

Servants get ahead because they are faithful. Timothy's reliability brought him to Paul's attention. Later, still young, he is head of the large and flourishing church in Ephesus. Paul is careful to tell Timothy to be respectful of the older men who are under his care.

How different things are in the world.

When was the last time someone got a big promotion in your company simply because he or she had faithfully done a good job? Of course people talk about how important it is to be dependable, reliable, and faithful. But the rewards usually go to those who are reliably aggressive, dependably glib with a line of talk, and faithfully adept at playing the game of company politics.

Dare I ask what qualities get people ahead in your church?

The rules are different in the Kingdom of

God for a very simple reason. There is nothing *we* can do for God. *He* is at work in the world. He can use us for his work if we adopt the attitude of a humble servant, listen to him, and do what he says. But we are useless to God if we cling to our worldly models of leadership and success. The gospel will go forth anyway. It doesn't depend on us.

But we talk as though it does depend on us. We see a talented executive, an energetic salesman, a charming teacher, a brilliant thinker, and we say, "If only *that* person were saved. Could *he* do a lot." But that's backwards. God doesn't need him. He needs God.

We say, "Wow, that is a creative person. He's full of good ideas. If only he would get saved and give his good ideas to the Kingdom." But God doesn't need good ideas. Eve was full of good ideas. God needs servants.

We go to a concert by a star entertainer who got saved, and we say "Wow, wasn't that spiritual?" Yes, but the spirit that is present isn't always the spirit of God.

We listen to a witness by some notorious public sinner who has been born again and we say, "Fantastic, that just shows how powerful the Lord is." But the Lord doesn't need the witness of a great sinner to prove his goodness. Neither do you. Look into your own past to understand the Lord's power to rescue great sinners from death. Look at the evil in your own heart this very moment to understand the greatness of God's love.

There are no superstars in the Kingdom of God. No chief executive officers. No flashy creative directors. No geniuses. No up-and-coming young men on the make. There are only servants whose eyes are always fixed on Jesus Christ. He is the model servant, the servant of the servants, the one who showed us how to serve by always doing the Father's will.

Stewards of the Mysteries of God

Too often, our service to the kingdom is lip service. Our lips say, "Of course I want to always be under God's immediate direction and control." Meanwhile, our minds say, "But if you really want to get something done, you've got to ..." What? Organise it. Run the numbers on it. Set up a committee to plan the job. Set up another committee to do it. Hire an administrator who will shape things up. Do some professional marketing. All this is done "in the Lord" of course, but often it's not in the Lord at all.

The brutal fact is that our flesh rebels against submission to God's authority and control. It *hates* being off centre stage. We are infinitely resourceful in devising a host of approaches and techniques that will allow us to appear to be doing one thing while doing another. We say

"Lord, Lord" with our lips while our hearts are wandering from him.

Paul was countering this worldly model of leadership when he wrote his letters to the church at Corinth. The Corinthians were thinking in terms of factions: who was in Paul's party, who was in Apollos's, who in Peter's? Who had the upper hand? Which party was really running the stewardship committee? Which faction was going to fill the vacancy on the school board?

"This is how one should regard us," Paul said sternly, "as servants of Christ and stewards of the mysteries of God."

We also are stewards. God's stewards conserve, preserve, and protect the gospel. They don't redesign the mysteries of God, improve on them, edit them, tinker with them. A faithful Christian steward becomes an instrument which God uses to proclaim the gospel. This is precisely what Paul did when confronted by the competitive Corinthians whose hearts were wandering from their master. He preached the gospel.

"Let no one boast of men," he wrote. "For all things are yours, whether Paul or Apollos or Cephas or the world or life or death or the present or the future, all are yours; and you are Christ's; and Christ is God's."

All things are ours. Forgiveness, salvation, eternal life. We belong to Christ. Preserve that mystery. Offer it to those who are hurting. It is more creative than your best idea. It contains infinitely more wisdom than your deepest insight. It brings more healing than your most solicitous care.

Take your place as a servant. Attend to the Lord, do what he tells you, be faithful, and let his power flow through you.

Also in this striking new series by John Wimber:

KINGDOM LIVING

In *Kingdom Living* John Wimber shows that 'being a disciple means more than just making a decision for Jesus and waiting for his Second Coming, it involves turning from sin, the flesh and the devil and becoming like Christ.' Pointing to the kingdom keys of worship, prayer, Scripture and a corporate life, Wimber stresses the need for obedience if we are to be Christ's imitators. The role of suffering in forming our kingdom character is discussed and John Wimber offers practical counsel on developing a Christlike character.

KINGDOM MERCY

'Our Christian walk,' states John Wimber 'begins with God's forgiveness and continues day by day in that same forgiveness.' Stressing the need for forgiveness to be given as well as received, Wimber looks at the danger of 'playing God' by deciding who, what and when to forgive. The prisons of bitterness and illness that can result from an unforgiving heart are sensitively portrayed as Wimber shares his own experiences with humour and insight. That God is gracious in his mercy and forgiveness is powerfully affirmed.